Ideas & recipes for

Lunches
and after school

snacks

CONTENTS

Published by Hyndman Publishing
PO Box 19, Amberley, North Canterbury

ISBN: 1-877168-37-8
TEXT: ©Simon & Alison Holst
DESIGNER: Rob Di Leva
PHOTOGRAPHY: Lindsay Keats
HOME ECONOMISTS: Simon & Alison Holst

The recipes in this book have been carefully tested
by the authors. The publisher and the authors have
made every effort to ensure that the instructions
are accurate and safe, but they cannot accept
liability for any resulting injury or loss or damage to
property, whether direct or consequential.

Because ovens and microwave ovens vary so much,
you should take the cooking times suggested in
recipes as guides only. The first time you make a
recipe, check it at intervals to make sure it is not
cooking faster, or more slowly than expected.

Always follow the detailed instructions given by
manufacturers of your appliances and equipment,
rather than the more general instructions given in
these recipes.

Acknowledgements

We would like to thank the firms who provided
us with the following food and products:

GOULBURN VALLEY Fruit in foil-topped pots
ALFRESCO Wraps (Mediterranean style breads)
from Quality Bakers
ALISON'S CHOICE Dried fruit, nuts, seeds, snack
foods, etc.
BENNICK'S POULTRY FARM, BULLER RD, LEVIN
Fresh eggs
EMPIRE FOODSTUFFS Dried herbs and spices
FARMER BILL'S Baby carrots
HARVEST MAID Dehydrators
LUPI Olive oil and Balsamic vinegar

Important Information

For best results, use a standard metric (250ml)
measuring cup and metric measuring spoons
when you use these recipes: 1 tablespoon
holds 15ml and 1 teaspoon holds 5ml.

All the cup and spoon measures in the recipes
are level, unless otherwise stated. Sets of
measuring cups make it easier to measure ¼
and ½ cup quantities.

Larger amounts of butter are given by weight.
Use pack markings as a guide. Small amounts
of butter are measured using spoons (1
tablespoon of butter weighs about 15 grams).

Abbreviations used:

ml	millilitre	tsp	teaspoon
cm	centimetre	Tbsp	tablespoon
g	gram	°C	Celsius

About This Book

Few of us jump for joy at the idea of organising and preparing packed lunches – but it is one of the facts of life that when our child starts school, we are probably letting ourselves in for more than TEN YEARS of cut lunches!

These lunches and snacks are important. If we want our children to enjoy school and perform well, we should ensure that they have plenty of fuel for physical and mental activity. Any teacher will tell you that a hungry child cannot concentrate!

Our aim in writing this book is to give you ideas and suggestions that will help you cope with all those years of lunch preparation, and help make the job less daunting!

Lunchtime at school will probably be the first time that your child eats food away from an adult's watchful eye. Instead of getting only messages about good nutrition, he/she will be influenced by classmates, not all of whom eat lunches that you approve of.

It is frustrating, to say the least, if your child returns home with the larger part of your carefully prepared lunch untouched. Without being defensive, try to find out why this has happened. Good communication here is vital! Perhaps you could look through this book together, until you find common ground.

Remember that the bottom line is to have your child eat something!

Find out how many different items your child would like, and pack small amounts of food in an appropriate number of separate packages, so they look inviting. Too much of each, or (surprisingly) too many options are daunting to a small child!

A traditional formula of a sandwich (or substitute), something based on fruit and/or vegetables, a snack or treat and a drink works well for many children. There are countless variations on this theme. You may want to add something for a mid-morning snack, or something to share with a friend.

Always encourage your child to eat a variety of foods, giving particular emphasis to fruit and vegetables. It has been shown that eating patterns established by the age of 11 or 12 are likely to persist through to the late teens or longer. A good lunch and worthwhile snacks make significant contributions to a balanced diet.

We hope that this book will help you make lunches and snacks that your child will enjoy, and make lunch preparation less of an ordeal!

Happy lunch-making!
Simon & Alison Holst

Containers for Lunches

You should be able to find a good range of lunch boxes, insulated containers, bags and drink containers, in a variety of stores. For the best selection, make your purchases at the beginning of the school year.

Before your child starts school, visit at lunchtime so that you can both see exactly what "everybody else" takes and eats, and what the lunch routine is. Peer pressure is considerable and many children want exactly what their friends have.

Look for drink containers which fit compactly inside lunch boxes if you want to freeze liquids in them. Buy several to keep in the freezer, if possible. Some sipper bottles, bought filled, are reusable.

Don't use breakable glass containers or inflexible lidded plastic beakers which crack and leak under pressure.

Make a collection of small, suitable, reusable containers with close-fitting tops, from delis, takeaways, etc.

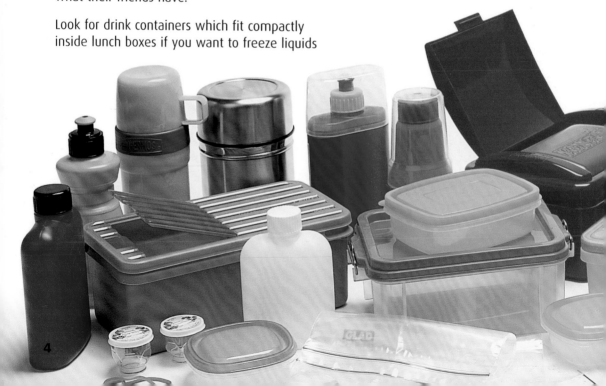

Mark containers clearly with your child's name or easily recognisable stickers, and explain what must come home, and what should be thrown away.

Explain the reasons for recycling and encourage children to discard as few reusable containers as possible.

Make sure that containers can be opened and sometimes reclosed securely by small hands.

Retrieve lunch containers promptly after school. Unpack and wash them thoroughly, as soon as possible, drain dry, and put them (with their lids) away where they will be ready for refilling. Store containers open rather than closed, to get rid of odours.

Most children like several small packages of different foods in their lunch boxes. Make a collection of tough plastic bags which seal tightly. Look for small resealable bags in stationers as well as supermarkets. Recycle bags where practical to do so. Some bags may be washed and dried for reuse.

Keep a drawer or other area in the kitchen for plastic bags, cling-film, scissors, markers that write on plastic, rubber bands, twist ties etc., so you can streamline lunch packing.

Lunch Tips and Hints

- Involve your child with lunch selections. Discuss options for the week's lunches, giving choices, and take the child shopping to choose some items such as fruit, nuts and snacks from bulk foods.

- Ask your child what he/she likes in friends' lunches and include these in return for your child eating something which you consider important.

- Don't insist on varying sandwich fillings if your child wants the same one every day. It isn't the end of the world! Introduce other fillings in sandwiches eaten after school, at home. Add variety with other lunch foods.

- Is it REALLY worth fighting about crusts on bread? Cut them off if it means that sandwiches will be eaten! (Cube and bake trimmings for croutons if you like.) Sandwiches cut out with a cookie cutter can be especially appealing.

- Don't include sandwich fillings or other foods which your young child has never tried before. Such "surprises" are seldom popular. Introduce new foods after school, at home, instead.

- Consider making deals with your child, for example, including a special treat or allowing a bought lunch on Friday if everything else is eaten throughout the week.

- If you don't function well in the mornings and hate a last minute rush, consider a different lunch-making routine. As children come in the door after school, get them to empty their lunch boxes straight away. Use unopened lunch items as part of after-school snacks. Clean lunch boxes straight away, then refill and refrigerate in the afternoon or evening.

- Get into the habit of cooking extra food for your evening meal – a bigger chicken, more hamburgers, another handful of rice or pasta. Afterwards, use extras as the basis of tomorrow's lunch, preparing, packing and refrigerating them straight away.

- If you have a freezer, spend an hour or so at the weekend doing the major part of lunch preparation for the week. Make sandwiches with freezable fillings (see next page), or pizzas, sausagemeat squares, pieburgers, etc. Make muffins or do other lunch baking, perhaps helped by your child. Wrap items as individual servings, label and freeze. Fill small zip-seal bags with various nutritious and interesting snacks such as popcorn, dried fruit, nuts, pretzels, etc.

- Sandwich fillings which freeze well include cheese spreads, mashed baked beans, spiced bean spread, peanutty chickpea spread, peanut butter, Marmite, sliced and grated cheese, cream cheese, raisins, chopped walnuts, date spreads, soft cheeses, ham, luncheon sausage and other meats, in slices or minced with chutney and tomato or other sauces. Do NOT freeze salad vegetables with any of these fillings.

- Don't run out of bread. Keep a loaf of sliced bread in the freezer. Separate slices with a pointed knife and spread frozen slices with sandwich fillings.

- Making lunches from basic ingredients saves money, but all children like bought items in their lunches at times. Choose good, nutritious bought items (like fruit pots) rather than packets of high-fat snacks. Save money by buying food in large containers or as bulk foods, and repackaging it in small ones. Reuse small sipper bottles that have been bought filled. Buy a large tube of potato crisps and include a few in a small zip-seal bag for a treat. Suggest that a child might open a sandwich and add a crisp to the existing filling before eating it. (Try this yourself – it is delicious.)

- Include non-edible surprises in lunch boxes occasionally. Add a note, riddle, joke, game, plastic toy or a puzzle made by cutting up a small card or picture.

- Bearing in mind that you may have twelve years of lunches to make, allocate a drawer or other area in the kitchen where lunch-packing equipment is kept. Keep a variety of sizes of zip-seal plastic bags, cling film, rubber bands, twist ties, sticky labels, stickers, marking pens, scissors, etc. in it.

- Consider having a whiteboard for shopping reminders for lunches, and a "lunch food" area in the refrigerator and freezer. Such things make it easier, too, when children pack lunches for themselves.

"I hate the filling falling out of my sandwiches as I eat them."

"Instant" Lunch Foods

Keep some of these on hand for days when you haven't got the time, ingredients or inclination to pack a sandwich lunch. Mix and match a number of the following items:

- Almonds
- Apple sauce/apple puree, small pots
- Apricots, dried
- Babybels or other mini-cheeses
- Bagel chips
- Banana chips
- Bananas, dried
- Breadsticks (small, dry)
- Cashew and other nuts
- Cheese, wrapped slices
- Flavoured milk (UHT–Tetra Pak)
- Crackers
- Crisp breads
- Dates

- Digestive biscuits
- Dips and crackers
- Dried fruit and nut mixtures
- Figs, dried
- Fruit fingers (fruit-filled biscuits)
- Fruit leathers
- Fruits in small pots, foil-topped
- Fruity Bix
- Juice boxes (Tetra Pak)
- Mediterranean crisps

- Milk, flavoured (UHT)
- Muesli bars
- Muesli mixtures
- Nuts
- Peanuts
- Peanuts & raisins
- Pita bread chips
- Popcorn
- Popcorn, coated
- Pretzels, peanut
- Pretzels, regular
- Prunes
- Puddings in pots
- Pull-top cans (macaroni cheese, baked beans, etc.)
- Raisins, little boxes
- Rice cakes
- Rice crackers
- Scroggin
- Snack logs
- Snack mixes from bulk bins
- Snippets
- Tiny biscuits, animals etc.
- Tuna/salmon, little tins of flavoured
- Walnuts
- Weetbix
- Yoghurt, raisins

Milk, Yoghurt and Cheese

Calcium-rich foods are important, so don't forget to include them in school lunches and after school snacks. Choose low-fat milk and yoghurts where you can.

Ways to add Milk

- "Bought" Flavoured milk, (freezable)
- Chocolate drinks, hot and cold
- "Bought" Smoothies, (freezable)
- Smoothies, homemade, (best fresh after school)
- Puddings in foil-topped pots
- Homemade custards, sago, etc.
- Canned rice and other puddings
- Homemade creamy vegetable soups

Ways to add Yoghurt

- Bircher Muesli, bought or homemade
- Homemade milkshakes and smoothies after school

Ways to add Cottage Cheese

Look for cottage cheese which your children like. (Cottage cheese made from full cream milk is still much lower in fat than "hard" cheese.)

- Eat alone with a spoon or with cooked fruit or icecream topping.
- Serve as a dip for raw fruit or vegetables.
- Stir into hot pasta (to eat cold).
- Stir into salads.

Ways to add Cheese

Look for lower-fat cheese varieties.

- Processed cheese squares
- Cheese spreads and dips (page 18)
- Grated cheese
- Mini cheeses, cubes and sticks
- Cheese-plus sandwiches
- Toastie pies, cold for lunch, hot after school
- Toasted cheese sandwiches

Swiss (Bircher) Muesli

This nutritious mixture makes an excellent complete meal, at any time of day.

FOR 2 SMALL OR 1 LARGE SERVING:
> 2–3 Tbsp chopped skin-on almonds
> 2–3 Tbsp chopped sultanas
> 1/4 cup rolled oats, fine or regular
> 1/2 cup low-fat, fruit-flavoured yoghurt
> 1/2 apple

Finely chop the almonds. Chop sultanas and add to almonds. Stir in the rolled oats and yoghurt. Remove core from quartered, skin-on apples, then coarsely grate or finely chop and stir into everything else. Refrigerate up to 24 hours. Pack in tight-lidded containers for lunches or eat as an after school snack.

Something to Sip

Children need plenty to drink.

- Water is a good drink! Make sure that a child starting school knows where the drinking fountain is, and how and when to use it.
- Water in a reusable bottle (especially a "sip-top" bottle) is often popular. Invest in several small sip-top bottles containing fruit drink, then refill them with water, diluted juice or diluted fruit cordial.
- In hot weather keep plastic bottles of drink in the freezer, putting them in the lunch box in the morning to chill the other foods.
- Freeze "bought" milk-based drinks in plastic bottles. (Home-made smoothies etc. are usually best drunk straight after making.)
- Liquids expand as they freeze. Don't overfill plastic containers. Squeeze sides before screwing on lids. Don't freeze glass containers.
- In cold weather, put hot drinks (e.g. hot chocolate) in vacuum flasks. Stock-based soups are filling as well as thirst quenching (page 27).

Orange or Lemon Cordial

Get ascorbic acid (another name for vitamin C) from a chemist, if necessary.

1 orange or lemon
1 cup each sugar and hot water
¾ tsp powdered ascorbic acid (Vitamin C)

Thinly peel skin from half an orange or lemon. Put in food processor with the sugar and ascorbic acid and chop finely. Add hot water and process until sugar dissolves. Add juice squeezed from the fruit, then strain out all "bits". Bottle and refrigerate up to 2 weeks. Dilute with water as needed.

NOTE: Vary the amount of acid to taste.

Quick Orange Drink

1 cup of orange juice makes 8 cups of drink!

¾ cup sugar
2 cups hot water
1 tsp powdered ascorbic acid (Vitamin C)
1 cup orange juice
about 5 cups cold water

Stir sugar, hot water and level measure of ascorbic acid together until sugar dissolves. Pour into a 2 litre (8 cup) jug. Add the orange juice, then fill with cold water. Shake before use. Refrigerate up to 3 days.

Keeping Your Lunch Cool

These days, with increasing concerns about food safety, there will be times when you want to keep packed lunches cool.

This is particularly true for some foods like eggs, chicken, cooked meat, and salads, especially in warm weather.

There are a number of different containers and/or methods you can use to keep lunches cool.

- Chill food and/or drinks overnight.
- Pack in insulated containers (thermos, bubble plastic, insulated bags/boxes).

- Pack freshly prepared food with a frozen lunch item, ie. drink bottle, Tetra Pak drink, foil-topped pots of fruit, grapes, muffins, baked items or even sandwiches*.

- Frozen items should thaw by lunchtime and keep other foods cool in the meantime.

- Keep a supply of reusable icepacks in your freezer. These come in various sizes, shapes and forms.

- Encourage children to keep their lunches in a cool place, out of sunlight, once they get to school.

* **NOTE:** Not all sandwich fillings will freeze well. Don't freeze sandwiches containing foods high in water, e.g., vegetables like tomato, lettuce, celery, etc. as these will make the bread soggy as they thaw. See page 7 for freezable sandwich fillings.

Use Your Loaf–Sandwiches and More...

For variety and fun, we use the term "sandwich" loosely! Think outside the square and don't limit yourself to conventional sliced bread. Experiment with breads. Wrap, roll, fill, fold or stuff various breads, using some of the fillings from the following pages. Enjoy the variety available! Look carefully in supermarkets and bakeries. Keep your eyes open for new products – and don't forget the variety of home-made breads you can bake.

- Thin sliced bread
- Thick sliced bread
- White bread
- White (high fibre) bread
- Wholemeal bread
- Fruit breads
- Multigrain bread
- Heavy multigrain bread
- Bread and dinner rolls
- Baps
- Hamburger buns

- Long (hot-dog) buns
- Currant buns
- French bread
- Pita/pocket breads
- Panini
- Focaccia
- Ciabatta
- Rewana
- Mountain breads
- Lavash
- Pizza breads

- Flour tortillas
- Naan breads
- Muffins
- English muffins
- Bagels
- Croissants
- Pikelets
- Crepes
- Pancakes

Wraps and Roll-ups

Large flat breads make wonderful wraps and roll-ups. Spread them with cream cheese, mayonnaise or leftover satay sauce, shredded lettuce or cabbage, grated carrot and cheese. Add a little cooked chicken, shaved ham, last night's leftovers, etc., for variety. Roll up firmly, and cut in manageable lengths. Keep cool (page 12–13).

Butter and Margarine Spreads

No one likes a sandwich that falls apart, but many "sandwiches" don't need butter or margarine to hold them together. Don't use high-fat spreads from force of habit, especially with fillings containing peanut butter, cream cheese, mayonnaise, etc. If you want them, or when they are necessary, use easy-to-spread products sparingly and look for salt and fat- reduced varieties.

Solo Sandwich Fillings

There's more to sandwich fillings than Marmite, cheese and peanut butter! The fillings can be used singly, although of course not all will suit all tastes. (Mixed fillings follow.) Remember that the bread alone makes sandwiches nutritionally worthwhile and that no sandwich is nutritious if not eaten! For larger appetites, use thicker slices of bread rather than more filling.

Savoury Sandwich Fillings

- Asparagus, freshly cooked or canned
- Avocado slices (with lemon juice)
- "Bacon bits"
- Bacon, cooked and crumbled
- Baked beans, mashed
- Bean salads
- Bean spreads (page 35)
- Beansprouts and alfalfa
- Beetroot (canned)
- Carrot, grated
- Cheese spreads (page 18)
- Cheese, processed slices
- Chicken, sliced or chopped
- Cold meat
- Coleslaw
- Corn chips, crushed
- Corned beef
- Cottage cheese, plain or flavoured
- Cracked wheat salads
- Cream cheese, plain or flavoured
- Cucumber, use telegraph, unpeeled
- Egg mixtures (page 18)
- Gherkins, chopped
- Grated cheese or soft sliced cheese
- Green and red peppers
- Ham
- Hummus
- Lettuce
- Luncheon sausage
- Marmite, etc.
- Mayonnaise (page 34)
- Meat loaf, sliced
- Meat pastes
- Mock chicken (page 19)
- Mushrooms, raw or marinated
- Nut butters
- Olives, chopped
- Pastrami, sliced or minced
- Patés
- Peanut butter
- Peanuts or other chopped nuts
- Pesto; basil, tomato, etc.
- Pickled vegetables
- Pineapple, crushed
- Potato crisps, crushed
- Potato salads
- Radishes, sliced
- Roast and barbecued meat
- Salami, thinly sliced
- Salmon, plain and flavoured
- Sardines, plain and flavoured
- Sausage; sliced, cooked
- Smoked salmon pieces
- Spaghetti
- Surimi
- Sweetcorn
- Taramasalata (page 35)
- Thinly sliced celery
- Tofu mixtures (page 19)
- Tomatoes
- Tuna, plain and flavoured

Sweet Sandwich Fillings

- Banana, mashed with lemon juice
- Chocolate chips
- Dates or date spread (page 19)
- Hazel-nut spread (page 19)
- Honey
- Hundreds and thousands (!)
- Jam
- Lemon honey
- Sultanas, etc., chopped

Interesting Filling Combinations

Here are some interesting ideas, using several ingredients. Use one or more of the suggested additions:

- Avocado (with lemon juice)/ tomato
- Apple/celery/chopped nuts/ mayonnaise
- Bacon/lettuce/avocado/ tomato (BLAT)
- Bacon/fried egg/lettuce/ rocket
- Bacon/lettuce/tomato (BLT)
- Baked beans (mashed)/ grated cheese
- Bean spread/cheese
- Cheese/chutney/relish/ pickles
- Cheese/crushed pineapple
- Cheese/gherkins
- Cheese/raisins
- Cheese/salsa
- Cheese spread (page 18)/ tomato/lettuce/sprouts
- Cheese/dates/orange rind
- Cheese/Marmite/lettuce

- or sprouts
- Chicken/chopped dried apricots/ cream cheese
- Chicken/cranberry/lettuce
- Chicken/lettuce/tomato
- Chocolate Hazelnut Spread (page 19)/bananas
- Chocolate spreads or chips/ sultanas or raisins
- Chopped or minced cooked meat/pickles/tomato sauce/shredded cabbage or lettuce
- Coleslaw/raisin/cheese
- Cooked (dried) beans, mashed/celery/spring onion/chilli sauce/ mayonnaise
- Cottage cheese/tomato
- Cottage cheese/banana/ honey
- Cream cheese/cucumber

- Cream cheese/pineapple/ grated carrot/raisins/grated cheese
- Cream or cottage cheese/ chutney/chopped gherkin/ beansprouts
- Cream cheese/chopped nuts/lettuce or alfalfa
- Cream cheese/chopped sultanas/nuts
- Cream cheese/lemon honey/nuts
- Crunchy peanut butter/ toasted chopped sunflower seeds/chopped sultanas/ honey
- Date spread (page 19)/ chopped nuts/grated cheese/cottage cheese/ peanut butter
- Egg (fried and chopped)/ bacon

- Egg/tomato/lettuce/sprouts
- Egg filling (page 18)/ cress/shredded lettuce
- Grated carrot/raisins/cheese spread (page 18)
- Grated or cottage cheese/ chopped celery
- Grated cheese/carrot/ celery/mayonnaise/raisins
- Grated cheese/chopped celery/spring onion/ mayonnaise
- Ham/cheese/cucumber/ lettuce
- Ham/coleslaw (or other salads)
- Ham/cream cheese/cottage cheese/pineapple
- Hawaiian: cheese/pineapple/shaved ham/lettuce
- Herbed Cream Cheese Spread (page 18)/lettuce
- Hummus/chopped olives
- Luncheon sausage/coleslaw
- Luncheon sausage/cheese/ tomato sauce
- Luncheon sausage (minced)/ chutney/salsa
- Pastrami/cream cheese/ rocket
- Peanut butter/banana
- Peanut butter/grated carrot/ cream cheese/chopped sultanas
- Peanut butter/cream cheese/ cottage cheese/alfalfa sprouts
- Peanut butter/bacon/ crushed crisps
- Peanut butter/mashed baked beans/bacon
- Peanut butter/tahini (in equal quantities)/mixed with honey or tofu/chopped sunflower seeds.
- Roast beef/tomato/relish/ lettuce
- Roast chicken/stuffing/ lettuce
- Salami/cream cheese/ avocado
- Salmon/cottage cheese/ lettuce
- Sardines/lemon juice/lettuce
- Sausage/tomato sauce
- Smoked salmon/cream cheese/horseradish
- Spaghetti (in tomato sauce)/ grated cheese
- Sweetcorn/relish/cream cheese/lettuce
- Tofu spread (page 19)/ lettuce/sprouts
- Tuna/mayonnaise/chopped cucumber/celery/spring onion

Additional Wrap, Roll and Pita Fillings
- Potato salads
- Rice or burghul salads
- Dips/spreads/chopped salad vegetables

17

"One Swipe" Sandwich Fillings

These are good made ahead and refrigerated for use over several days. Use them alone, without butter or margarine, or with other fillings (pages 16–17).

Tangy Cheese Spread

Melt 50g butter with 1–2 tsp flour and ½ tsp Dijon mustard in a pan, stirring all the time. Add ¼ cup milk and stir until mixture bubbles and is smooth. Stir in 1 cup (about 100g) grated tasty cheese and ½ tsp vinegar, taking off heat as soon as cheese melts. Refrigerate up to a week.

Savoury Cheese Spread

Mix together 2 cups grated tasty cheese, ½ cup evaporated (unsweetened) condensed milk and half a 30g packet onion soup mix, a few hours before needed. (Mixture thickens on standing.) Refrigerate up to a week.

Cheese and Onion Spread

Heat 1 cup water and a 30g packet onion soup mix together, stirring until thick. Remove from heat and add 2 cups grated cheese. Stir until cheese melts. Refrigerate up to a week.

Herbed Cream Cheese Spread/Dip

100g soft butter or margarine
2 cloves garlic, chopped finely
¼ tsp each salt and sugar
freshly ground pepper
2 Tbsp chopped chives
¼ cup chopped parsley
2 tsp fresh thyme
250g carton (lite) cream cheese
2 Tbsp lemon juice
2 Tbsp milk

Mix first 8 ingredients well, using a fork or food processor. Blend in cream cheese, lemon juice and milk. Refrigerate in a covered container up to 2 weeks.

Egg Sandwich Filling

4 (warm) hard-boiled eggs, peeled
2 Tbsp milk
1 Tbsp room temperature butter or margarine
¼ cup finely chopped chives, spring onion and/or parsley
¼ –½ tsp salt
pepper to taste

Put everything into a food processor and process until smooth, adding salt and pepper to taste. OR mash warm eggs with a fork, then mix well with everything else, seasoning to taste. Cover and refrigerate up to 4 days.

VARIATIONS: Add curry powder to taste. Replace milk and butter with mayonnaise.

Tofu Sandwich Filling

This looks and tastes like egg filling.

250–300g firm tofu
3 Tbsp mayonnaise
1 tsp mild mustard
¼ tsp turmeric
¼ tsp salt
2 Tbsp chopped parsley and chives
1 Tbsp lemon juice (optional)
black pepper to taste

Crumble drained tofu into a bowl. Gently stir in everything else and mix well to coat tofu. Season to taste. Refrigerate up to 2 days.

Mock Chicken

1 onion, finely chopped
1 Tbsp oil
2 Tbsp water
1 firm tomato, finely chopped
1–2 Tbsp mixed fresh herbs
1 egg, beaten with fork
salt

Put onion, oil and water in a small non-stick pan. Cook with lid on until onion is wilted and water absorbed, then cook uncovered, without browning for 2 minutes longer. Stir in tomato and herbs, cook 2 minutes longer, then add egg and cook gently as for scrambled egg, just until egg is set. Season to taste. Refrigerate up to 2 days.

Chocolate Hazelnut Spread

1 cup hazelnuts
2 Tbsp caster sugar
100g cooking chocolate
2 Tbsp oil

Bake hazelnuts at 180°C for about 10 minutes, or until the nut flesh is very lightly browned, then rub in a teatowel to remove the dark skins. While still hot, finely chop nuts in a blender or food processor with the caster sugar. Melt chocolate with oil in a pot taking care not to overheat, then add to the nuts and process until fairly smooth. Keep at room temperature up to several weeks.

"Creamy" Low-fat Date Spread

1 cup dates, finely chopped
½ tsp cinnamon
½ tsp mixed spice
¼ cup low-fat or non-fat yoghurt,
  plain or flavoured
½ cup skim milk powder

Put everything in a food processor. Process with metal chopping blade until smooth, thinning with extra yoghurt if necessary. Refrigerate in a covered container up to a week.

Turning Spreads into Dips

Thin spreads with more of the liquid used in the recipe, or with (hot) water, until they are of dip consistency.

Make Your Own Pizzas

There are many options when it comes to making pizzas! Most simply add toppings to a bought pizza base, pita bread, split bread rolls or English muffins, and bake. OR prepare your own base from thinly rolled scone dough (mix 2 cups self-raising flour and ½ tsp salt with 1 cup milk and 2 Tbsp oil), or make a bread base (see below).

TOPPINGS: These days almost anything goes for pizza toppings but for packed lunches, simple seems best! Spread chosen base/s with tomato mixtures (Mix 2 Tbsp each tomato paste and water, with 1 tsp oreganum.) or use bought pizza topping or canned spaghetti!

Next, add 3 or 4 of the following:
- A little thinly sliced onion
- Thinly sliced red/green/yellow peppers
- Sliced mushrooms
- Sliced or diced ham/bacon, salami, sliced cooked sausage, shredded chicken, etc.
- Anchovies and/or chopped olives
- Well drained canned corn or pineapple
- Chopped fresh or dried basil, thyme, etc.

Finish with a generous layer of sliced, grated, or crumbled cheese (mild or tasty cheddar, mozzarella, feta, or a mixture).

Bake at 200°C for 10–15 minutes, until base has browned underneath, or grill toppings on bread rolls or pita bread.

Easy Bread Base
(for 1 very large, 2 medium, or 8 individual bases)

2 tsp active dried yeast
1 cup plus 2 Tbsp warm water
2 tsp sugar
1 tsp salt
2 Tbsp olive or canola oil
3 cups high grade flour

BREAD MACHINE DOUGH: Measure everything into bowl, set to dough cycle and start machine. Check dough after 5 minutes, mixing to see if it has formed a smooth ball. Add a little extra flour or water, if required. Shape as described below.

HAND-MADE DOUGH: Measure the first 5 ingredients and 1 cup of flour into a large bowl. Mix until well combined. Cover bowl and leave for 15 minutes. Stir in remaining flour (adding extra, if necessary) to make a dough just firm enough to knead. Knead for 10 minutes, then cover and rise in a warm place until doubled in size. Shape as below.

TO SHAPE: Turn dough onto a floured surface and divide as required, then roll each piece into a circle, 5–7mm thick. Place on pizza pan or baking sheet, then add toppings and bake as described on page 20.

Calzone & Stromboli

If you make your own bases, try these "closed" pizzas.

CALZONE: Arrange pizza fillings on one half of individual base/s, leaving 2cm uncovered at edge. Moisten edges, then fold the uncovered half over the filled half to make a 1/2 moon shape, pressing the edges together. Bake like a pizza.

STROMBOLI: Roll dough into a large, very thin rectangle/s. Top like pizza (use toppings sparingly), then roll the dough up like a spring roll. Slash the top diagonally a couple of times to prevent splitting, then bake like a pizza. Serve sliced in short lengths.

▼ (FROM LEFT TO RIGHT)
After School Specials (page 22), Mum's Mousetraps (page 23), Individual Pizzas (page 20), Stromboli (page 21), Calzone (page 21), Pizza (page 20) and Toastie Pies (page 22)

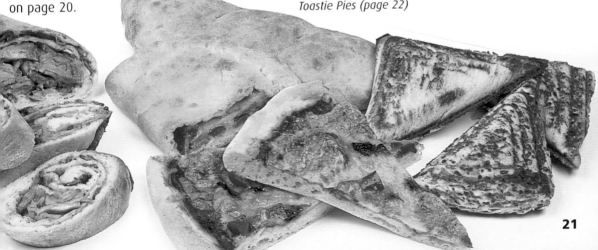

After School Specials

These grilled savouries make great after school snacks or weekend lunches. Try them cold in packed lunches, too.

> *3 bread rolls, halved, or 6 slices bread*
> *1 large egg*
> *½ cup creamed corn*
> *1 cup grated cheese*
> *2–3 spring onions, finely chopped*

Toast cut rolls or bread until lightly brown on both sides.

Mix the egg, corn, cheese and spring onion if using, in a bowl with a fork. Spread mixture over the toasted rolls or bread, right to the edges (to stop edges burning).

Grill, not too close to the heat, until golden brown and bubbly.

VARIATIONS: Add ¼-½ cup of one of the following:

- Canned baked, Mexican or chilli beans
- Canned spaghetti
- Canned or leftover mince mixtures
- Whole kernel corn
- Well-drained crushed pineapple
- Chopped salami or luncheon sausage
- Chopped leftover vegetables, well drained
- Canned tuna mixtures
- Chopped, drained sardines
- Chopped new potatoes

Melba Toasties

These use up stale bread and make a wonderful aroma to come home to!

Heat oven to 150°C (fan-bake for first choice). Cut stale sliced bread, flour tortillas, other softish flat breads, pita breads, etc. into fingers, rectangles, triangles or any fancy shapes you like. Cut bread rolls into thin slices. (Separate the two halves of pita breads.)

Spray lightly with canola, olive or other oil spray. Sprinkle lightly with garlic salt or any seasoning mixture, if you like, OR leave plain.

Place bread pieces close together on an oven tray or cooling rack. Bake until quite dry and golden brown. Very thin tortillas and very stale bread cook fastest. Start checking after 4 minutes. Thicker, fresher bread may take 10–20 minutes. Keep checking! Store in airtight containers when cold. Refresh for a few minutes after storage, if you like. Eat plain or use for dipping.

Toastie Pies

Heat the toastie pie maker. For each toastie pie, lightly spread two slices of bread with butter or margarine, right to the edges. Mix filling, using a filling from the "After School Specials" recipe (page 22).

Put one slice of bread, spread side down, in the hot appliance. Spoon in some filling (not too much) and put the other piece of bread on top, spread side up. Close the machine and cook following manufacturer's instructions.

Eat almost straight away or cool on a rack before wrapping in paper towels and packing in a lunch box.

Toasted Cheese Sandwiches

Good on a cold day, after school!

Spread butter or margarine thinly on two slices of stale bread. With buttered sides *out*, make a sandwich of thinly sliced cheese, with tomato sauce, salsa or chutney if you like, but with no extra butter.

Carefully place in a preheated frying pan on medium heat, and cook until golden brown, then turn with a fish-slice and cook the other side. Cut into halves or quarters and eat straight away.

Mum's Mousetraps

Popular for after school snacks, and useful in packed lunches on mornings when you run out of time.

> *1 medium sliced loaf*
> *500g grated tasty cheese*

Put halved bread slices close together on oven trays lightly sprayed with non-stick spray. Sprinkle evenly with the cheese.

Bake at 150°C for about 60 minutes, until completely dry and crisp. If cooking several trays at once, change their position every 10 minutes after half an hour. Cool on a rack. Store in airtight plastic bags or jars. Keep up to 2 weeks.

"I want some things bought from stores in my lunch box."

Pieburgers

Versatile, delicious and always popular!

1 egg
500g minced beef
¼ cup tomato sauce
2 Tbsp flour
30g packet onion soup
½ cup grated tasty cheese
2 sheets pre-rolled pastry (150g each)
Parmesan cheese (optional)

Heat oven to 200°C. Break egg into a large bowl and beat to mix. Pour half egg into a cup and put aside. Mix mince, sauce, flour, soup and cheese in the bowl with half egg.

Roll the thawed pastry thinly on a floured bench to make two 23–35cm squares. Divide meat into nine equal blobs. Put in three rows of three on one sheet of the pastry. Brush pastry with cold water. Lie the other sheet of pastry on top. Using a rolling pin, press pastry layers together between mounds. Cut along pressed edges to make nine parcels. Trim edges and cut an air vent on each pie. Brush with reserved egg. Decorate with trimmings if you like.

Put on baking tray. Bake 30 minutes, until golden brown. Cool on rack. Eat while fresh or freeze.

Sausagemeat Square

This square contains fruit and vegetables – it's a good way to 'hide' them!

450–500g sausagemeat
1 large egg
1 tsp curry powder (optional)
2 Tbsp tomato (or plum) sauce
1 large onion
1 medium-large apple
1 medium-large potato
1 large carrot
½ cup grated cheese

Heat oven to 170°C. Mix sausagemeat, egg, curry powder and sauce in a large bowl. Grate the onion, unpeeled apple, and scrubbed, unpeeled potato and carrot, then mix them evenly through sausagemeat mixture.

Press mixture into a 23cm square baking pan lined with baking paper. Sprinkle with the cheese and bake for 45 minutes, until firm in the centre. Cut into 9–12 pieces. Refrigerate or freeze for lunches.

▼ (FROM LEFT TO RIGHT)
Stuffed Eggs (page 26), Pieburgers (page 25), Sausagemeat Square (page 24) and Self-Crusting Corn Quiche (page 26)

Self-Crusting Corn Quiche

FOR 4–6 SERVINGS:

4 eggs
1 cup milk
½ cup self-raising flour
½ tsp salt
425g can creamed corn
1½ cups grated tasty cheese
up to 2 cups chopped cooked potatoes,
  kumara, broccoli etc., (optional)

Heat oven to 220°C. Beat first four ingredients together in a bowl or food processor until mixed. Sir in the corn and 1 cup of the grated cheese and pour into a buttered or sprayed 20cm square tin.

OR if you like, and have them, add any other well-drained cooked vegetables, chopped no bigger than 1cm cubes. Mix briefly and pour into a 23cm buttered or sprayed square tin.

Bake for 20–30 minutes or until the centre is firm. Leave for 10–15 minutes, then cut into squares or rectangles. Serve warm or cold in lunches. Freeze individual portions.

Stuffed Eggs

2 eggs
1 tsp butter or margarine
salt and pepper to taste
curry powder or herbs (optional)
about 1 tsp milk

Tap a tiny hole in the rounded end of each egg with a metal skewer to stop shell splitting. Boil for 12 minutes. Cool eggs in cold water, then peel.

Halve eggs and remove yolks. Mash yolks with butter, optional seasonings and enough milk to make a smooth, soft mixture. Spoon filling into egg whites. Wrap securely in cling film.

Cook extra savoury (non-bread) foods the night before, refrigerate overnight and pack in lunches. Keep them cold in warm weather (page 12).

Try: chicken drumsticks and nibbles
  cold, baked or barbecued sausages
  hamburger patties
  meatballs or rissoles
  samosas
  spanish omelet
  frittata
  schnitzels
  lamb chops

Winter Warmers – Flask Fare

On chilly days some children love the idea of taking a flask of hot food for lunch.

Choose a wide-mouthed plastic or stainless steel vacuum flask, and explain that it needs to be treated with care!

Get into the habit of cooking larger amounts of suitable "flask foods" when making dinner. Refrigerate leftovers and reheat the next morning. Mince and vegetable mixtures, chili beans, pasta dishes and 2-minute noodles fortified with extra vegies are likely to be popular.

Soup and sandwiches make popular cold weather lunches. Use your favourite cans or packets, or start from scratch.

To keep foods hotter longer, preheat the flask by filling it with hot water until you are ready to fill it with hot food. Preheat foods in a microwave in a covered container. For even heating, use a lower power level and a longer time.

Fifteen Minute Alphabet Soup

FOR 4–6 SERVINGS:
- 4 cups hot water
- 2 tsp instant chicken stock
- 1 tsp each sugar and butter
- ¼ cup alphabets (or 1/2 cup larger pasta)
- 1 small onion, finely chopped
- 1 stalk celery, chopped
- 1 small carrot, grated
- 1 small potato, grated
- 1 Tbsp chopped parsley (optional)

Boil the water in a pot. Add the instant stock, sugar, butter and pasta. Prepare and add each vegetable in the order given. Add the grated potato when everything else is almost cooked, since it thickens the soup.

Quick Pumpkin Soup

FOR 2–3 SERVINGS:
- 1 cup (about 150g) cubed pumpkin
- 1 tomato, chopped
- 1 cup water
- ½ slice stale bread, cubed
- 1 tsp instant green herb or chicken stock
- 1 cup milk
- 2 Tbsp grated cheese (optional)

Simmer pumpkin and tomato in the water for 7 minutes, or until cooked. Stir in bread and stock. Puree mixture, adding milk, and cheese if you like. Reheat without boiling. Serve, or pour into a thermos flask. Eat with "Mousetraps".

Salads to Go

Salads make a good addition to packed lunches. Substantial salads may replace sandwiches. The following salads may all be made ahead and refrigerated overnight. Make sure they are packed in leak-proof containers.

Rice and Corn Salad

1 tsp Dijon mustard
2 tsp wine vinegar
1 Tbsp olive or other oil
1 cup (leftover) cooked rice
1 stalk celery, chopped
1 chopped spring onion (optional)
3–4 radishes, chopped
¼ cup canned or frozen corn
1 Tbsp chopped parsley

Mix mustard, vinegar and oil together and stir into rice. Add finely chopped vegetables, corn and parsley. Mix and refrigerate in a tightly closed container.

NOTE: Frozen corn thaws by lunchtime.

Carrot and Apple Salad

Grate a carrot and a tart apple (Cox's Orange, Sturmer, Braeburn or Granny Smith). Mix with enough mayonnaise to coat (1–2 Tbsp) and add sultanas, chopped walnuts or roasted peanuts if you like. Mix gently.

▼ (FROM LEFT TO RIGHT)
Potato Salad (page 29), Oriental Noodle Salad (page 30), Peanutty Rice Salad (page 29), Pasta & Tuna Salad (page 28) and Tabbouleh (page 30)

Peanutty Rice Salad

½ tsp sesame oil
1 Tbsp canola or other oil
1 tsp light soy sauce
1 cup (leftover) cooked rice
¼ -½ cup frozen peas
¼ -½ cup chopped roasted peanuts
¼ -½ cup grated carrot
2 Tbsp chopped parsley, spring onion or other fresh herbs (optional)

Mix first three ingredients in a bowl or plastic bag, then add everything else. Shake or stir to mix. Refrigerate until required. Carry in tightly closed containers.

NOTE: Peas thaw by lunchtime.

Pasta and Tuna Salad

2 Tbsp mayonnaise
2 tsp lemon juice
1 Tbsp olive oil
½ tsp salt
1 firm tomato, diced
½ cup chopped cooked green beans
3–4 black olives (optional)
½ can plain tuna (drained) or 1 small can flavoured tuna
2 cups cooked pasta shapes
1–2 Tbsp chopped fresh parsley
1 small hardboiled egg

In a large, shallow bowl, stir together the first 4 ingredients. Add everything else except the egg and toss gently. Put the quartered hardboiled egg on top.

Oriental Noodle Salad

FOR 2-4 SERVINGS:
  2 cups water
  1 packet 2-Minute Noodles
  1 Tbsp wine vinegar
  2 Tbsp oil
  1 cup finely shredded cabbage
  1 carrot cut in thin strips
  2 stalks celery, thinly sliced
  1–2 spring onions, sliced

Boil water in a pot. Add broken noodles. Boil for 2 minutes then drain. Mix flavour sachet contents, vinegar and oil, and stir into warm noodles with the prepared vegetables.

Nice additions include: ¼–½ cup chopped peanuts, or ½–1 cup of cooked chicken or ham with a sprinkling of sesame oil and soy sauce.

Coleslaw

Put leftover coleslaw in filled rolls or in small tight-lidded containers.

Finely shred quarter of a cabbage and coarsely grate a scrubbed carrot. Toss together with your favourite bought dressing or a dressing made by shaking together 2 Tbsp oil, 1 Tbsp wine vinegar, 1 tsp each sesame oil and sugar and about ½ tsp salt.

Nice additions include: grated cheese, chopped roasted peanuts, toasted seeds and nuts, thinly sliced celery and/or spring onions, small cubes of unpeeled apple tossed in lemon juice, sultanas or raisins.

Tabbouleh (Bulgar and Tomato Salad)

FOR 4–6 SERVINGS:
  1 cup bulgar (burghul)
  2–3 cups boiling water
  2 spring onions, chopped
  ¼ cup lemon juice
  ¼ cup olive oil
  ½–1 cup chopped parsley
  ¼–1 cup chopped mint
  2 cups cubed tomato (see below)
  salt, pepper and sugar to taste

Pour boiling water over the bulgar. Leave for 30 minutes. Drain by pouring into a sieve lined with a clean cloth, then gather up and twist ends of cloth to force out excess water.

Toss drained bulgar in a bowl with the next five ingredients. To prepare tomatoes, halve them, shake out the seeds and juice. Chop. Add them to the salad 30 minutes before serving. Season to taste.

Serve at room temperature. Refrigerate until required. Carry leftovers in tightly closed containers for lunches.

VARIATION: Replace bulgar with couscous. Use 1½ cups boiling water and stand for 6 minutes. Do not drain.

Ten Minute Salmon and Couscous Salad

FOR 2–3 SERVINGS:

1 can (100-200g) salmon
1½ cups liquid (see below)
½ tsp minced chilli (optional)
¾ cup couscous
2 spring onions, chopped
1–2 cups chopped cucumber
2 stalks celery, chopped
fresh herbs
1 cup chopped firm tomatoes
juice of 1 lemon
2–3 Tbsp olive oil
salt and pepper to taste

Use whatever sized can of salmon you have. Drain liquid from it and make up to 1½ cups with chicken stock. Add the chilli and bring to the boil.

Sprinkle in the couscous, take off heat, cover and leave for 6 minutes.

Meantime, chop all vegetables except tomatoes into a shallow salad bowl. Add herbs if available.

Toss the salmon through the room-temperature couscous with half the lemon juice and oil. Season to taste then fork through the vegetables, toss gently with the remaining lemon juice and oil, and top with the tomatoes. Refrigerate/pack leftovers in tightly closed containers for lunches.

Basic Vinaigrette

2 Tbsp wine vinegar or lemon juice
about ½ cup olive or canola oil
1 tsp Dijon or mild mustard
salt, sugar and pepper to taste

Put all ingredients in a jar and shake to mix. Refrigerate up to 2 weeks.

Potato Salad

Slice or cube cooked new or waxy potatoes into a bowl. For each 2 cups of potato, add a chopped spring onion, ½ cup sliced celery (optional), 2 tablespoons chopped parsley, ¼ cup mayonnaise (thinned to pouring consistency with a little lemon juice or milk), 1 teaspoon wine vinegar and 2 chopped hardboiled eggs. Mix gently.

If cooking pasta the night before, add an extra handful and refrigerate leftovers. For a quick lunch salad, add sliced luncheon sausage, ham, tuna, or cottage cheese, and diced cooked vegetables or cubed salad vegetables. Toss with vinaigrette or your favourite dressing.

Ways to Add More Vegetables to Lunches and Snacks

Recent figures suggest that children are not eating nearly as many vegies as they should. Encourage them by trying some of the following appetising ideas for lunches, after school snacks, or as TV "munchies" in the late afternoon. Check out the selection of interesting dips for raw vegetables (page 34). Try to keep a selection of chilled raw vegetable pieces and strips in airtight plastic bags, within easy reach, in the refrigerator at all times. Add vegies to cheese, meat, egg, tuna, etc., in sandwiches, where possible.

Raw Vegies, Alone or As Dippers

- Asparagus
- Bean sprouts
- Beans, small tender green, in short lengths
- Broccoli
- Carrot sticks
- Carrots, whole baby
- Cauliflorets
- Celery sticks

- Corn cobs, cut in pieces after cooking
- Cucumber sticks, without seeds
- Mushrooms, button
- Peas, snow or sugar snaps
- Pepper strips, red or yellow
- Radish, long white (daikon) in slices or strips
- Radishes, tender young
- Swede, in strips
- Tomatoes, especially cherry
- Turnip, young white, in quarters
- Zucchini sticks

Other Ways with Vegies
- Asparagus rolls
- BLT sandwich
- Other sandwiches (pages 15–17)
- Cherry tomatoes and cottage cheese
- Coleslaw (page 30)
- Frozen peas/corn in pasta or rice salads (pages 28–29)
- Grated cheese and carrot together
- Lettuce rolls filled with cheese
- Salads to go (pages 28–31)
- Stuffed celery (with cheese fillings, page 18)
- Vegetables and dips (pages 34–35)
- Vegetables in soups (page 27)
- Vegies in cakes and muffins (pages 44–45)

Vegies to Dip

It is fun to dunk small strips or pieces of crisp vegetables in a dip before eating them. Introduce your child to this idea, and to the dips themselves, at home before dinner or as a TV snack. Pack vegetables for dipping in tightly sealed plastic bags or small leak-proof containers. Pack dips in screw-topped or other leak-proof small containers. (Note: Wash prepared dipping vegetables just before packing them, since the residual water keeps them crisp. DO NOT add salt.)

Creamy Dip

½ cup mayonnaise
½ cup lite sour cream
½ tsp celery or onion salt
¼ tsp garlic salt
1–2 tsp chopped fresh herbs

Stir all ingredients together. Refrigerate up to a week in a covered container.

Good Old Onion Dip/Spread

Mix together 1 packet (about 30g) onion soup and a 250g carton low-fat or regular sour cream until smooth. Refrigerate up to 4 days, thinning with milk or yoghurt if dip thickens too much on standing.

VARIATIONS: Replace half or more of the sour cream with plain, unsweetened yoghurt. Add finely chopped herbs or nuts.

Mayonnaise for Dips/Spreads

1 large egg
½ tsp each salt and sugar
1 tsp Dijon or mild mustard
2 Tbsp wine vinegar
about 1 cup olive or canola oil

Measure everything except oil into a food processor bowl. Process, dribbling in oil. The more oil you add, the more the mixture thickens. Refrigerate, covered, for up to 2 weeks.

Peanutty Chickpea Dip/Spread

300g can chickpeas, drained
¼ cup peanut butter
finely grated rind and juice of 1 lemon
1 clove garlic, crushed
1 tsp ground cumin
3 Tbsp olive oil

Puree everything in a processor or blender, thinning with 2–4 Tbsp can liquid, water or plain unsweetened yoghurt to spread or dip consistency. Refrigerate up to 3 days.

Spiced Bean Spread/Dip

1 Tbsp canola oil
1 small onion, chopped
1 clove garlic, chopped
1 tsp dried oreganum
1 tsp ground cumin
¼ -½ tsp chilli powder
400g can baked beans, drained
salt to taste

Cook first six ingredients over low heat for about 5 minutes. Add drained beans, cook for 2–3 minutes longer, then mash or puree in a blender or processor, thinning to spread or dip consistency with reserved bean liquid. Season, adding lemon juice or tomato paste, if you like. Refrigerate up to 4 days.

Taramasalata Dip/Spread

50g smoked cod's roe
3 thick slices stale bread
½ cup milk
1 small onion, finely chopped
¼ cup lemon juice
about 1 cup olive or canola oil

Chop roe coarsely, discarding papery skin. Put the roe and broken bread into processor, pour milk over bread and leave several minutes to soak. Add onion, then process the mixture until smooth. With the motor going, add the lemon juice, then dribble in oil. The more oil you add, the more the mixture thickens. Refrigerate up to a week.

"Instant" Peanutty Dip

The easiest dip we know, good for apple slices and vegetable sticks or pieces.

2 Tbsp peanut butter
2 Tbsp orange juice
1 tsp honey

Mix together until smooth and creamy. Taste and alter proportions, if you like.

Corn Cobs

Microwave corn cobs, uncovered, in their husks, 2 or 3 at a time, for 3 minutes per cob on High (100% power). Leave for 1 minute or longer, then remove husks, cut cobs into two or more pieces, and wrap. Dip in mayonnaise or eat plain.

"I want lunch that's just the same as everybody elses."

Ways to Add More Fruit to Lunches and Snacks

Encourage children to eat fruit (and fruit products) regularly. Pack inviting fruit (and/or fruit products) in every lunchbox and have more within easy reach after school.
Listen to your child's comments and check the following:

- Is fruit ripe enough (and sweet enough)?
- Is fruit small and easily managed?
- Is it packed so it won't leak, drip or brown?
- Are you sure it won't be messy to eat?
- Will kids need a paper napkin or wet wipe?
- Have kids tried it at home first?
- Is it different from yesterday's fruit?

Fruit To Go!

- Apples, small whole, or cubed in orange juice
- Apricots, dried or fresh
- Bananas, small fresh or dried
- Dates, plain or stuffed with cheese or cheese spread (page 18)
- Dried fruit mixtures
- Feijoa halves, with teaspoon
- Fresh cherries
- Grapes, seedless, fresh or frozen
- Kiwifruit halves, ripe, with teaspoon
- Mandarins

- Melon cubes
- Nectarines, whole or cubed in orange juice
- Orange segments
- Passionfruit, halved, with teaspoon
- Pineapple cubes
- Plums
- Prunes, plain or flavoured
- Raisins, small packets
- Strawberries, whole or halved, lightly sugared
- Tamarillos, ripe, in halves or as fruit leather

Other Ways with Fruit
- Apricot balls (page 41)
- Dehydrated fruit, homemade or commercial

- Fresh fruit salads, lightly sugared or in orange juice
- Fruit in cakes and muffins (page 38–45)
- Fruit juice
- Fruit rollups
- Fruit sago or tapioca
- Fruit set in jelly
- Fruit to dip* with little forks/toothpicks
- Fruit yoghurt
- Mini fruit kebabs: grape, pineapple, cheese on toothpicks
- Pots of fruit (foil topped)
- Smoothies (pureed fruit and yoghurt)

* **DIPS FOR FRESH FRUIT:** Fruity yoghurt, vanilla or chocolate custards, dairy foods, cottage cheese, fruit purees, mayonnaise.

Muffins, Other Baking and Treats

Nearly all children like something sweet in their lunches. Here are some of our favourites – most of them are 'worthwhile' without going overboard!

A B C Muffins

A for apple, B for banana, C for chocolate.

1 cup (2–3) mashed ripe bananas
½ cup brown sugar
¼ tsp salt
¼ cup canola oil
1 large egg
½ cup milk
½ cup chocolate chips
1 apple, grated or finely chopped
2 cups self-raising flour

Heat oven to 200°C. In a large bowl, mix together the mashed banana, sugar, salt, oil, egg and milk until well mixed. Stir in the chocolate chips and the unpeeled apple which has been coarsely grated or chopped in a food processor.

Shake the flour through a sieve on to everything else and fold together until just dampened. Spoon into 24 mini-muffin pans or 12 medium muffin pans. Bake for 10–12 minutes or until golden brown.

OPTIONAL LEMON GLAZE: Mix 2 Tbsp each lemon juice and sugar. Brush over hot muffins.

Blueberry Bran Muffins

1 cup baking bran (wheat bran)
¼ cup wheatgerm or extra bran
½ cup canola oil
¾ cup plain or fruity yoghurt
1 large egg
1 tsp cinnamon
¾ tsp salt
1 cup sugar
1–1½ cups frozen blueberries (150-180g)
1½ cups plain flour
1 tsp baking soda

Heat oven to 200°C. Measure the first eight ingredients into a medium-sized bowl, mix well with a fork, then leave to stand.

Separate clumps of frozen blueberries, then stir into bowl. Shake in the flour and soda through a sieve, then fold through. If mixture looks dry, add ¼ cup extra yoghurt or milk.

Spoon into 12–15 medium or about 30 mini-muffin pans which have been well sprayed. Bake for about 15 minutes, until centres spring back when pressed.

OPTIONAL LEMON GLAZE: Mix 2 Tbsp each lemon juice and sugar. Brush over hot muffins.

Simon's Spiced Fruity Muffins

1 cup wholemeal flour
1 cup plain flour
4 tsp baking powder
½ cup sugar
½ tsp salt
2 tsp cinnamon
2 large eggs
½ cup canola oil
2 x 140g pots fruit in juice
½ cup raisins or sultanas
½ cup chopped walnuts (optional)

Heat oven to 200°C. In a large bowl, mix the first six ingredients. In another bowl, beat eggs with a fork. Add oil and fruit (with juice). Fold into dry ingredients with the dried fruit and walnuts, until just dampened. Spoon into 24 mini-muffin pans or 12 medium muffin pans. Bake for 10–12 minutes or until golden brown.

Double Chocolate & Banana Muffins

2 cups self-raising flour
2 Tbsp cocoa
½ cup sugar
½ cup chocolate chips
½ tsp salt
¼ tsp baking soda
1 cup (2–3) mashed bananas
¼ cup canola oil
¾ cup milk
1 large egg
1 tsp vanilla

Heat oven to 210°C. In a large bowl, mix the first six ingredients together with a fork. Mash bananas, put in a bowl with the remaining ingredients and mix well. Fold liquid mixture through dry ingredients until flour is dampened, stop before mixture is smooth. Do not over-mix.

Spoon into 12 medium or 24 mini-muffin pans coated with non-stick spray. Bake for 10–15 minutes, until centres spring back when pressed.

Champion Cheese Muffins

2 cups (200g) grated tasty cheese
1½ cups self-raising flour
½ tsp salt
1 Tbsp sugar
1 large egg
1 cup milk

Heat oven to 210°C. Measure grated cheese, self-raising flour, salt and sugar into a large bowl. Mix together with fingertips.

In a small bowl, beat egg and milk with a fork until evenly combined. Pour liquid onto dry ingredients, then fold the two mixtures together, without over-mixing.

Spoon into 12 medium or 24 mini-muffin pans sprayed with non-stick spray. Sprinkle with a little extra cheese if you like. Bake for 10–12 minutes, until muffins spring back when pressed in the middle and are golden brown.

Pikelets

Sandwich these together with jam or honey for lunches, or eat after school.

25g butter or margarine, melted
1 household Tbsp golden syrup
1 Tbsp sugar
½ cup milk
1 large egg
1 cup self-raising flour

Heat a frypan. (Use a high heat setting if frypan is electric.) Put melted butter in a fairly large bowl, add golden syrup and stir to mix. Beat in sugar, milk and egg. Add flour then mix with a beater just until smooth.

Cook in spoonfuls in an oiled, heated frypan. When first bubble bursts on each pikelet, flip over. Second side is cooked when centre springs back when pressed. Pile warm pikelets in a plastic bag.

Note: If mixture does not spread, stir extra milk into the batter. Raise or lower heat if the pikelets are too light or too brown when turned.

Boiled Fruit Loaf

Sandwich 2 slices of this loaf together for lunches. Good after school, too.

For 1 loaf (about 10x23cm):
1 cup water
¾ cup sugar
1 cup sultanas
25g (2 Tbsp) butter or oil
2 tsp mixed spice
½ tsp salt
1½ cups plain flour
1 tsp baking powder
½ tsp baking soda

Heat the oven to 170°C. In a medium-sized pot, boil then simmer first six ingredients (uncovered) stirring occasionally, for 5 minutes. Important: Stand pot in cold water to cool to room temperature.

Meantime, line sides and bottom of loaf tin with two strips of baking paper. When mixture in pot is cold, sieve in remaining dry ingredients, and stir just enough to blend.

Bake 45–60 minutes, until centre springs back when pressed and a skewer comes out clean. Slice when cold or freeze for later use.

▼ (FROM LEFT TO RIGHT)
Blueberry Bran Muffins (page 38), Pikelets (page 40), ABC Muffins (page 38), Almost-Anzac Biscuits (page 42), Apricot Balls (page 41) and Double Chocolate & Banana Muffins (page 39)

Apricot Balls

Rind from ½–1 orange
½ cup caster sugar
250g dried apricots, chopped
¼ cup orange juice
about 1¾ cups fine desiccated coconut

Remove orange rind with potato peeler and finely chop it with the sugar in a food processor, then add apricots and finely chop in bursts. Add orange juice and process again.

Add a cup of the coconut, process, then add more until mixture sticks together nicely. With wet hands, shape into small balls and roll in remaining coconut.

Refrigerate until firm. Store in refrigerator or freezer.

Almost-Anzac Biscuits

100g butter
¼ cup golden syrup
½ –1 tsp vanilla or almond essence
1 cup sugar
1 cup rolled oats
1 cup coconut
1 cup plain flour
½ tsp baking soda
2 Tbsp warm water

Heat oven to 160°C. Melt the butter in a fairly large saucepan. Add golden syrup and stir until blended. Take off heat. Add next five ingredients to the saucepan. Stir everything together then add baking soda dissolved in the water and mix again.

Using your hands, shape into walnut-sized (or smaller) balls, flatten slightly and place on baking-paper lined trays, leaving room for spreading. Bake for about 15 minutes, until evenly golden brown.

Transfer to a rack after 1–2 minutes. When cold, store in airtight containers.

Variation: Add 1 cup chopped roasted peanuts with sugar, etc. If mixture is crumbly, add 1–2 Tbsp extra water.

Scroggin Lunch Biscuits

This recipe makes the equivalent of nearly six 200 gram packs of biscuits!

200g butter
¼ cup peanut butter
½ cup sugar
1 cup (packed) brown sugar
2 large eggs
1 tsp vanilla or almond essence
1½ cups plain flour*
1 tsp baking soda
2 cups rolled oats
1 cup chocolate chips
1 cup sultanas
½ cup chopped walnuts

*Use ¼ cup less flour if using instant rolled oats.

Heat oven to 180°C. Mix the softened butter and the next five ingredients together in a large bowl, then stir in the flour and baking soda. Add everything else and mix, using a wooden spoon or your hand.

Shape with two spoons or put flattened rounds of mixture on baking-paper lined trays, leaving space for spreading. Bake in batches for about 12 minutes or until lightly browned then cool on a rack.

Gingernuts

Great for lunch boxes and after-school snacks, with a glass of milk.

100g butter
1 household Tbsp golden syrup
1 cup sugar
1 large egg
1¾ cups (200g) plain flour
2 tsp ginger
1 tsp baking soda

Heat oven to 180°C. Melt butter in a pot. Stir in a rounded household tablespoon of syrup. Take off heat and beat in the sugar and egg with a stirrer or wooden spoon.

Shake dry ingredients through a sieve into the pot. Stir to mix. Arrange small spoonfuls (or balls) of warm mixture on sprayed or oiled trays, leaving space for spreading.

Bake for about 10 minutes, until lightly browned. Cool on rack and store in airtight jars. Popular in lunches and particularly good with a glass of milk, after school.

NOTE: Measure flour carefully. Biscuits don't spread if you have used too much flour. If you don't use enough, they spread too far.

Chocolate Chip Cookies

75g butter
½ cup (packed) brown sugar
½ cup white sugar
1 large egg
½ cup chocolate chips
½ tsp baking soda
1 cup plain flour

Heat oven to 180°C. Melt butter then beat in both the sugars and egg using a fork. Add chocolate chips, sift in the soda and flour, then mix together.

Line two trays with baking paper. Place 12 spoonfuls of mixture on each tray, leaving room for spreading.

Bake for 8–10 minutes until golden brown. Cool on a rack. Store cool biscuits in airtight containers. Use in the same way as gingernuts.

"I hate chopped up fruit that goes brown."

Yummy Zucchini Chocolate Cake

125g butter
1 cup (packed) brown sugar
½ cup white sugar
3 large eggs
1 tsp vanilla
½ cup yoghurt (any type)
2½ cups plain flour
3 cups (350g) grated zucchini
¼ cup cocoa
2 tsp baking soda
2 tsp cinnamon or mixed spice
½ tsp salt
½ cup chocolate chips

Heat oven to 170°C. Line bottom and sides of a 25cm square pan or roasting pan with two crosswise strips of baking paper.

Beat softened butter with sugars in a mixer or food processor until light and creamy. Mix in eggs, vanilla, yoghurt and ½ cup of the measured flour, then mix in grated zucchini. Sift in remaining flour and next 4 ingredients. Stir gently, then pour into the pan. Sprinkle with chocolate chips.

Bake for 45 minutes, or until centre feels firm and a skewer comes out clean. Cool on rack. Refrigerate, or freeze wrap pieces.

Food Processor Apple Cake

2 medium apples (preferably tart)
1 cup sugar
1 large egg
100g butter, melted
1 cup plain flour
1 tsp cinnamon
1 tsp mixed spice
pinch ground cloves (optional)
1 tsp baking soda
½ cup chopped walnuts

Heat oven to 180°C. In a food processor with a metal chopping blade, chop the quartered, unpeeled apples into pieces the size of peas. Quickly add the sugar, egg and melted butter, and process to mix through the apple.

Measure remaining ingredients on top of apple mixture. Mix briefly, using pulse button, then spoon into a 20cm square tin lined with two strips of baking paper.

Bake for 45–60 minutes, or until the centre springs back and a skewer comes out clean. Leave for 5–10 minutes before turning out. Dust with icing sugar before serving.

Pineapple Carrot Cake

1 cup wholemeal flour
1 cup plain flour
1 cup sugar
2 tsp cinnamon
1½ tsp baking soda
1 tsp salt
½ cup chopped walnuts
2 cups (250g) grated carrot
3 large eggs
1 cup canola oil
1 tsp vanilla
225g can crushed pineapple

Heat oven to 160°C or 150°C fan-bake. In a large bowl, mix the first eight ingredients. In another bowl, beat the eggs, oil, vanilla and pineapple (including liquid) with a fork. Stir both mixtures together, mixing until just combined.

Pour into a 23cm square baking pan lined with 2 strips of baking paper. Bake for about 45 minutes until centre feels firm and a skewer comes out clean.

Leave for 5–10 minutes before turning out. Ice when cool if desired.

OPTIONAL CREAM CHEESE ICING:
Beat together until creamy 2 Tbsp cream cheese, 2 Tbsp room temperature butter, ½ tsp vanilla and 2 cups icing sugar. Spread over cooled cake and sprinkle with chopped walnuts.

▼ (FROM LEFT TO RIGHT)
Crispy Popcorn (page 47), Chocolate Nut Brownies (page 47), Yummy Modelling Dough (page 46), Pineapple Carrot Cake (page 45), Scroggin Lunch Biscuits (page 42) and Butterscotch Fingers (page 46).

Butterscotch Fingers

125g butter
½ cup sugar
1 large egg
1 tsp vanilla
1 cup self-raising flour
1 cup plain flour

Filling:
100g butter
2 household Tbsp golden syrup
400g can sweetened condensed milk

Heat oven to 170°C. Cut the butter in to 9 pieces and warm in a large pot until starting to melt. Take off heat and beat in the sugar, egg and vanilla. Stir in flours until crumbly, then squeeze into a ball, using your hands.

Line a shallow 23x33cm tin with baking paper. Break ¾ of dough into bits (and chill remainder) and pat evenly over base of tin.

Melt second measure of butter. Add rounded spoonfuls of syrup and stir in the condensed milk. Mix, then pour over unbaked base in tin. Coarsely grate chilled dough on top.

Bake for 30–45 minutes until crust is golden and filling has browned. Leave 2 hours. Cut into fingers with a sharp knife dipped in hot water. Refrigerate or wrap and freeze individual pieces.

Chocolate Truffles

100g wine biscuits, crumbed
100g butter
¼ cup cocoa
1 cup icing sugar
½ cup coconut
¼ cup chopped walnuts
¼ cup chopped sultanas
2 Tbsp orange juice (or sherry)

Crush biscuits in a plastic bag using a rolling pin. Soften, but do not melt the butter. Stir in everything else. Cool mixture in refrigerator until firm enough to roll into small balls with damp hands. Roll in extra coconut. Refrigerate or freeze up to 2 months.

Yummy Modelling Dough

You can make ½ or even ¼ quantities of this delicious edible play-dough.

4 Tbsp creamed honey
8 Tbsp smooth peanut butter
12 Tbsp non-fat dried milk

Mix everything in a large bowl or food processor, with the metal chopping blade or a wooden spoon, then your hands. Cut into 20–30 pieces and put in small "zip-shut" plastic bags (2 pieces in each).

Refrigerate up to two weeks. Pack in lunches with a message to share with a friend, or play with it after school. (Wash hands first!)

Chocolate (Nut) Brownies

Until you have made these, you won't realise how easy they are and how good they taste!

125g butter
¼ cup cocoa
1 cup sugar
2 large eggs
¼ tsp salt
1 tsp vanilla
1 cup plain flour
1 tsp baking powder
½ cup chopped walnuts (optional)

Heat oven to 180°C. Melt butter until liquid in a medium-sized pot then take off heat. Using a fork, mix in the cocoa, sugar, eggs, salt and vanilla. Sift in the flour and baking powder, add the chopped nuts if you like, and stir until evenly mixed.

Pour into a 20–23cm square tin lined with baking paper. Bake for about 30 minutes, or until firm in the centre. (Don't worry if mixture is higher at the edges than the middle — it still tastes fine!)

Cut in pieces when cold. Freeze for lunches.

Crispy Popcorn

Popcorn makes a great healthy snack food!

FOR 6 CUPS POPCORN:
Put ¼ cup of popping corn and 1 Tbsp canola oil in a large pot or pan, preferably with a glass lid. Cover and heat, shaking the closed pot every 30 seconds or so. After a few minutes corn will start to pop. Turn heat low, and keep lid closed to stop hot corn popping out of pan! Shake pot at intervals.

When all popping has stopped, open the pot, keeping small faces away. Serve as it is, or flavour it.

FOR BUTTERED POPCORN: Drizzle 1 Tbsp each melted butter (or margarine) and canola oil over hot popcorn in the pan and toss to coat evenly.

FOR CHEESY POPCORN: Shake 3 Tbsp grated Parmesan through hot buttered popcorn.

FOR CINNAMON POPCORN: Mix ¼ cup icing sugar and ¾ tsp cinnamon. Shake over hot buttered popcorn with ¼ cup each sultanas and roasted peanuts. Mix well.

Eat straight away (after school) or pack in tightly sealed plastic bags for lunches.

"I hate butter spread too thick in my sandwiches."